# Under the Shimmering Light

SHEWLI GHOSH

# DEDICATION

I swam to show support for my grandmother, a
courageous breast cancer survivor who showed me the
"Art of Living Brave"

My swim is a tribute to her and other cancer survivors to
commemorate their silent strength, hope, resolve and faith.

# CONTENTS

# ACKNOWLEDGMENTS TO

My parents and brother Shiv who supported me all the way

Aunt Manisha who introduced the sport to my dad and me

Cousins Samir and Viraj who encouraged me throughout while joking with me every step of the way

Grandparents who gave me their support, showed their concern and prayed for me

Swim coaches

School principal, teachers and friends in Platte River Academy (PRA) who encouraged me

A special shout out to Bill Wygant of South End Rowing Club (SERC) who made this swim possible by trusting me and allowing me to undertake this swim at ten years of age.

# 1 INTRODUCTION

Writing this book has been a milestone in my thirteen years as I have grown with this momentous event. I am presenting this honest account of my experience, putting forward all my skills learnt so far. I have written this remembrance to share my very unique journey of swimming for a little over an hour in the cold waters from Alcatraz Island to the Aquatic Bay in San Francisco, a distance of 1.25 miles.

When I was four, my grandmother had been diagnosed with breast cancer. She battled through harsh treatment, and I heard about her ups and downs as I was growing up. Thinking of the possibility that breast cancer may be genetic brought this reality close to me. The thought that I might get it when I grow older scared me and I am not scared easily. Because others are going through this very fear of the disease, I wanted to do something big to measure up to the sacrifice and fight that women go through to battle this disease.

I first swam Alcatraz when I was ten years old. I wanted to show solidarity and respect to the most inspiring breast cancer survivor - my grandmother. The cause of my swim was to spread the word of "Early detection is the key to fight Breast Cancer." I trained hard, met the coolest people, and received loads of support for my cause.

Before and during the swim I battled against my fears of monsters in the sea, self-doubt, and my own active imagination. I had to push all these "10 year old demons" aside before jumping into a grey, murky, and angry body of water they called the sea to complete this swim.

*My "10 year old demons"*

There is a huge thrill, challenge and allure in open water swimming. After training in the pool, open water swimming is like learning how to swim again. Without temperature-controlled chlorinated water, lane dividers or starting blocks, it's like a whole new world. There are finishing times that average one to two hours, fluctuating elements and the occasional kick or elbow to the face from other swimmers. Since you can't see an arm's length away from you, having a big imagination doesn't help in this scenario.

This book is to introduce my readers to my experience of frigid open water swimming and to give a better understanding of this sport.

I have also included training tips for swimming in the cold seas and dealing with strong tides for those who may undertake a similar swim like the Alcatraz Invitational. I have learned these techniques from various trainers, my dad, other seasoned swimmers, and of course the Internet. GOOGLE! Just remember, like Scar, Simba's uncle said in the movie, *The Lion King* said, "BE PREPARED!!!!!!!!!"

In addition I have talked about some of the best seafood and coolest sites that I had the chance to see during my short visits to the Bay Area.

Push aside all your fears and take the plunge with me through my adventure of escaping THE ROCK.

# 2 ARE THERE SHARKS IN THE BAY?

Everyone always asks the question, "Are there sharks in the Bay? Yes, there are sharks along with sea lions, jelly fish, big fish, cold temperatures, and fast moving motor boats in the Bay.

But seriously, sharks are the least of your worries when you are swimming cold open waters like the murky bay in San Francisco.

*Yum! Breakfast is Served!*

Before swimming the frigid waters of San Francisco, I did a little research that showed me around 11 species of sharks found in the Bay itself. The cool waters of Northern California are prime Great White Shark habitat. In fact, the threat of shark attack was regularly used to dissuade criminals from trying to swim from Alcatraz Island when it was being used as a maximum security prison.

So to answer the next question, is swimming in the Bay dangerous? I would say YES. Any fast moving motor or sailboats would be the most dangerous thing to watch for when swimming outside of the Aquatic Park cove.

*A container ship in the channel where we swim*

As the water is at a temperature of 55 to 65 degrees Fahrenheit, hypothermia can be lethal. So learning the symptoms of hypothermia and respecting your limits in the cold water would be the best approach to recognize and deal with it.

Sea lions have taken up residence on Pier 39 and the surrounding waters and are a big tourist attraction. Sea lions have been known to bite, but this is rare. On my third swim, I came face to face with an inquisitive Sea lion.

*My close encounter with a cute Sea lion*

Contact with multiple jelly fish and getting stung by their slimy tentacles while in the waters all cause potential hazards to a swimmer.

On the next page is a very amusing email that put my fears into perspective. We received it just before the swim from the SERC.

♦♦ Start of Email ♦♦
From: SERC
Sent: Wednesday, September 9, 2009 2:06 PM

Subject: 2009 SERC Alcatraz Invitational Swim

On September 12, 2009 at 8 am The South End Rowing Club will be asking 600 of our closest friends to jump off a perfectly good boat 'abeam' Alcatraz Island into the San Francisco bay and swim back to our club at Aquatic Park. Approximately 26 minutes later the fastest swimmer will be on the beach and headed for breakfast prepared by club members. The club actually has two Alcatraz swim records, one for the summer and one for our New Year's Day Alcatraz Swim. The summer Alcatraz swim record is still held by Joel Wilson, coach of the Santa Cruz Masters is under 19 minutes and we are still wondering how he did it. Another long time Alcatraz record is held by Bob Placak for a swim out and around Alcatraz Island and back to the clubhouse in 1 hour 6 Minutes. The record for the fastest swim by a human is held by Tom Jaeger who swam a 50 yard swim in Nashville Tenn. in 1990 in what works out to be 5 mph.

Now timing the speed of sharks has been difficult. They are normally thought to cruise at around 1.5 mph; the short-fin Mako shark is considered the speediest of the shark family and has been timed at 25 mph with short bursts of speed of up to 43 mph. Great White Sharks are thought to swim at sustained speeds of 25 mph, especially if they are hungry. The Farallon Islands is only a 58 minute swim from San Francisco for a Great White Shark. Heck I've driven that to get to a place I heard had good hamburgers, wouldn't you?

Now we are fairly confident there are no Great White Sharks in the San Francisco Bay, they were known to follow whaling vessels looking for food as far as the Sacramento River during the 1800's. For the most part sharks are carnivorous and primarily eat meat. However the one thing we feel sharks really hate is the thought of eating vegetables. Shark moms have for eons been trying to get their young pups to eat more greens and root vegetables to balance out their diet, but without much success. However it's generally just meat, meat, meat, with these top apex predators, whose size can reach over 20 feet.

But we've recently found a pill that seems to make human's taste like a vegetable. We will be selling this shark repellant pill at our swim for $5. We're not sure if they really work, but we feel it's better to err on the side of caution when dealing with a predator the size of a Great White Shark.

All proceeds from the sales of our shark repellant pills will be donated to the City of Hope and used for cancer research.

"...the greatest enjoyment of life is to live dangerously . . . Just don't forget to take your shark pill." Friedrich Nietzsche.

♦♦ End of Email ♦♦

As you might guess, the pills were flying off the shelves. Little did my dad know that I didn't need the pill, I had no way of being harmed by a Great White Shark. You see I had read somewhere and seen on TV maybe, that sharks can identify a fatter prey and go for a higher "FAT PER BITE" ratio. So, I made my dad promise that he would swim close to me (not too close) and always be next to me during the whole swim. See, my own form of shark bait!

*View from the breakwater to Alcatraz Island*

*View from the breakwater to Aquatic Park*

# 3 ALCATRAZ

What is the lure and mystery about Alcatraz Island? And why was it an inescapable prison facility? I wanted to see and learn more about it myself. Before leaving for San Francisco, my dad and I watched two Hollywood movies. *Escape from Alcatraz* starring Clint Eastwood and *The Rock* with Sean Connery and Nicholas Cage. These gave me a Hollywood perspective about the island and why it was considered inescapable. I learned more when I toured the prison confines with my family. I would say the combination of the movie, the ferry ride to the Island and the prison tour were awesome. I knew what to look for when the tour guide pointed out the happenings within the well-fortified prison walls.

Something that the tour guide mentioned made me feel compassion for the prisoners. He mentioned that on certain days, like major holidays, the inmates could clearly hear the sounds of the city, music and laughter from their cells. I can just imagine how torturous their existence within the confines of the prison would feel, and harboring a constant desire to escape. The city lights and the sounds must have made freedom seem so attainable yet so far away.

A study of history books, online articles and Wikipedia came up with a few more curious facts. Found in the center of San Francisco Bay, the infamous Alcatraz Island. The Island is also known as "The Rock", is a well-known yet mysterious place containing many forgotten memories and lost ghosts. Though no one really knows everything that went on within the concealed walls of the old prison, it still manages to trap the interests of millions of people who visit the national park on the small island in the San Francisco Bay. Not only has it trapped the interests of those numerous visitors, but it had also captured my imagination.

*My first image of the ROCK*

Discovered in 1775 by a Spanish explorer named Juan Miguel de Ayala, La Isla de los Alcatraces was nothing more than a small island inhabited by a group of pelicans from which the island acquired its name (Alcatraces means pelicans in Spanish). It wasn't until the Spanish-American War in 1898 that the United States realized that the isolation of the island made it an excellent candidate for a prison. The prison population jumped from twenty-six to 450 during the war. That number sprang once more after the famous 1906 earthquake when prisoners were transferred from many San Francisco city jails to Alcatraz. With the island becoming more a prison and less a military fort, it was decided that cell hoses would be necessary and beneficial. After the construction of the cell house in 1912, "The Rock" was born.

In the 1920's many inmates were allowed to own small gardens of their own. Baseball fields were created and small teams were formed. It wasn't until the 1930's that Alcatraz went through dramatic changes constituting stricter rules than ever before thus ending the days of gardening and baseball games. In 1963, however, due to the high cost of running an island prison, Alcatraz was officially closed, never to be reopened as a prison.

*Alcatraz Island on a calm day, it looks so close!*

The ownership of the Island kept changing as it was repurposed multiple times through history. Finally, the

U.S. government decided it would be best to make Alcatraz part of the newly opened Golden Gate Park. Today, the money it attracts from its visitors each year provides the operational costs for the island.

*A view of the San Francisco sky line*

Throughout all the change, Alcatraz has experienced, it has retained one thing up its deteriorating walls never cease to capture the amazement and interest of onlookers like you and me.

*A view from Alcatraz when I was 10 in 2009*

This small, haunted and mysterious island on the coast of San Francisco holds so many memories and such a rich history that it will always be referred to as a personality more than a geographic location. "The Rock" is legendry, and I proved one of its myths wrong by swimming to shore from it at the age of 10.

*Google Earth of Alcatraz Swim to the Aquatic Park*

# 4 THE SWIM

2009, September 12th 4:30 am, as I woke up the skies indicated that we would be in for an adventure. The city's famous fog was already making plans to roll down the mountains and create a misty chill in the air. I could see drizzle on the car windshield and occasional flashes of lighting in the distance as we drove away from my cousins house to San Francisco Bay. The drive through dark, windy roads and freeways bathed in misty fog brought me closer to the point of no return. I was painfully aware that my actions would have to live up to my big mouth. We reached the South End Rowing Club at the corner of the Fisherman's Warf by 6am.

The Fisherman's Warf in the early morning light looked so peaceful. Bathed in an eerie twilight with all the regular businesses closed for the night, we had the streets to ourselves. Isn't that great? The area looked a lot larger and less menacing.

At the South End Rowing Club (SERC), we (my dad, aunt, and I) stood in one of the lines that were set up for swimmer registrations and check-in. The volunteer at the check-in tents gave us our race packages and timing chips. Given the number 197, it made me think of being tagged as a criminal. The gentleman who stood in line behind us was from the Australian Navy and on vacation. Who would go on a vacation for this? Oh, wait, I did. I was supposed to be at school this morning, I changed into my wetsuit, got body marked (the number I was given had to be written on my exposed skin) and waited for the swim briefing. There was a 'sea' of nervous and smiling faces, all in anticipation of their performance in the choppy seas. Though the veteran swimmers tried to cheer us up, all that I thought about was, "How am I going to do this without being a disappointment?" It was a very boisterous crowd who greeted each other. They called out to friends, and prepared for the swim. Folks changed out of their street clothes and transformed themselves into wetsuit- clad black penguins; some brave souls wore only their swim suits ready to conquer the cold waters of the Bay. There were about 600 swimmers of various nationalities and age groups trying to accomplish the same feat that morning. The race director Bill Wygant stood at the entrance of the SERC balcony and addressed the crowd over a bull horn.

A hush fell over the crowd as every swimmer paid close attention as if their lives depended on it. To me it seemed like it did. We all got our instructions and guidance on the water conditions, tide timings, prominent structures in the city skyline to use for sighting, and a few last minute tips. There was apprehension on people's faces as they made tweaks to their swim plan based on the information just provided.

After the briefing all swimmers walked in a group, building up an encouraging, happy and festive atmosphere for all who were going to swim. We walked towards Pier 33 to board the Blue & Gold ferry. This would transport us to the start line, a few yards from the island of Alcatraz.

*With dad. Notice my anxious eyes!*

The walk to Pier 33 was very memorable as we followed a distinguished looking gentleman dressed in a Scottish kilt and playing a lively marching tune on the bag pipes. We all followed him as if being led by the famous pied piper. It was such a unique feeling, with everyone chatting, laughing and exchanging names and an occasional joke.

*The Bagpiper of San Francisco   Can you see him behind me?*

At Pier 33 we all crowded around the ferry entry gangway waiting our turn to board. There were a lot of pictures being taken and last minute encouragements from friends and relatives who had to stay behind.

*śubh yātrā – Safe Journey in Hindi*

The bagpiper continued his clarion call to all the brave

swimmers, most of whom did not know what was in store for them.

*The Blue & Gold ferry*

Looking around there were athletic looking women and men in various color wetsuits, mostly black. There were people of all sizes and colors from ruddy old guys in speedos and huge bellies to svelte young ladies with colorful swimsuits. My dad asked a rather big, rosy cheeked guy in a really skimpy speedo, if he was concerned about the cold water. That guy roared in laughter and remarked, "You call this cold water? You should come and swim in Ireland to know the meaning of cold." He said he welcomed this warm 50 + degree waters of the Bay. He had flown down specially to swim the Alcatraz as it was on his 'to do list' to swim these fabled inescapable waters. I looked around and saw a beautiful lady wearing a shimmering swimsuit and I asked myself the question why were people wearing black color wetsuits and shimmering swimsuits as if to mimic seals or swimming schools of fish. I looked down at my wetsuit, it had just a small blue logo on it and the remaining was black. Like a seal with one blue eye.

*Queue to board the Blue & Gold ferry*

All of a sudden there was a surge towards the ferry. We had started the boarding process. I walked with dad. My mother and brother got special permission to accompany us on the ferry for moral support. As it was our turn to step on the gangway, my mother and brother were asked to step aside to allow all the swimmers to board first.

*Mustering up courage as I am nervous and uncertain*

I immediately felt a great separation anxiety and started feeling apprehensive as my security blanket was being taken away from me. My dad squeezed my shoulder and encouraged me to continue boarding and reassured me that my mother would join us soon on board. I felt nervous, and uncertain of the swim that I was about to undertake. Is it just me or is anyone else's throat dry? I wanted to get a drink of water badly, that privilege had to wait as we were already in our wetsuits and water would increase the chances to wanting to visit the restroom on the ferry. Funny, feeling thirsty while being surrounded by water.

*You can feel the tension*

On board we were all packed in like sardines, I wanted some space to take this moment in, so we found a corner table to sit down. There was a huge roar from all the swimmers and people at the wharf as the ferry gave a loud blow of its horn and we were away. I looked around my, eyes welling up with big tears as I could not see my mom. I looked at my dad who was busy engaged in a conversation with another swimmer. I looked around feeling lost, and a huge knot of anxiety started growing in my stomach. Suddenly, I felt a tap on my shoulder; I whipped around to see the smiling face of my brother, and lifting my eyes I saw my mother's familiar face. I ran into her warm embrace and held on tight. I nervously chatted with my brother and mother and looked over at my dad who was still chatting with another swimmer. Little did he know that I was getting the jitters and cold feet about the swim.

*The seas look rough!*

All sorts of thoughts were racing through my mind as I looked out at the rain and wind-splattered port hole. The swells seemed to be quite high; the skies were grey as if crying its heart out in a gentle drizzle accompanied with occasional lightning in the distance. Just like myself - I was crying inside, doubting myself as never before. I thought,

"What if I can't make it to the other side? What if the water is so cold that I would freeze up? What if …"

I was the youngest swimmer on board that day and there were others on board who were drawing inspiration from me. They all wanted to know how old I was and where I lived. The conversations got me going and I stopped feeling so weird about the swim. I chatted with my mom and played a quick game of rock paper scissors with my brother.

*Swimmers on the ferry awaiting the big JUMP*

All of a sudden the ferry started slowing down. Next, it cut its engines and came to a gradual halt. It was time to make the jump. The knot in my stomach came right back.

Last minute instructions were blared out over the loud speakers about the jump. There would be two sides of the boat that we swimmers could jump from and we would jump in pairs or threes. Someone would be at the door to clear us for the jump.

*I am crying inside*

We got into the queue to make the jump. dad took it all in and whispered into my ear to hold my swim goggles against my face when we jumped, bob up as soon as possible and to swim away from the sides of the ferry immediately to avoid being jumped on. He said that as soon as we were a few strokes away from the boat we would regroup and then start the swim.

As we were gently pushed forward by the crowd, I looked back at my mother once more and could see her look of concern and brave face. I could imagine that sending your daughter into such a huge challenge in rough weather could not have been an easy decision. I remember my mother telling my dad to be by my side for the entire swim and look after my wellbeing. I saw them exchange a brief look of trust, strength and reassurance.

We were suddenly standing at the edge of ferry side and being encouraged to take the jump. My dad and I had paired up and it was just us jumping together. WHAT IN THE WORLD WAS I DOING? I looked out at the sea. It was rough with high swells. The rain caressed my face, and it felt cold. There was no turning back now. I knew I was ready. I had prepared in the lakes of Colorado, and I had swam the distance with my dad next to me. I heard, "You are next. Jump and clear the area, Good Luck, You can do it!"

I jumped, doing just what we had decided to do. I held my goggles against my face and stepped off the side. I could hear my dad giving out a tribal whoop as we accelerated to the waiting cold. Due to the rolling of the ship and high swells, I think we must have jumped about eight to twelve feet before hitting the water feet first. As I plunged into the icy waters, I kept going under with the momentum. I must have gone about six to eight feet before, my mind screamed to me to stop my descent and head back to the surface. Talk about a massive brain freeze. This was different. In addition to a ten ton hammer slamming on my head, all my exposed skin on my face, wrists, fingers, ankles and toes were almost flash frozen.

Bobbing up from the jump, I wanted to take a gasp of life-giving air. My dad had warned me about this, and I waited just a second before taking that breath. It gave me a chance to figure out where I was in relation to the sea surface and waves so I took a gulp of air rather than sea water. I touched my face to check if I still had my goggles on.

I saw my dad come up next to me; he quickly brought me back to reality. We took a few moments to get oriented and he pointed to the two buildings we wanted to use for sighting. Once we had that sorted out, we stuck out for the Aquatic Park landing 1.25 miles away.

I knew I had to swim away from the boat in order to avoid getting jumped on, but my body was still in shock. As I started to swim, ice cold water seeped into my wet suit drop by drop. Parts of my body started freezing up to the sudden exposure of cold H2O. It felt like a vampire was sucking every last drop of warmth out of my body. For the first time in my life, I felt like the skin of my face was peeling off.

As I swam, I knew I was slowly getting colder and colder so I knew I had to speed up. In a pool that would be easy but the San Franciscan water does not yield much to you and has a very chilly embrace. The short practice swim I did the day before couldn't have prepared me for this plunge into the water from such a height and the effects of cold after that or the crazy weather or rough waters. The swells were huge, the wind and rain were making the waves very unpredictable. My goggles started to fog up my vision and I stopped for the first time. Apparently, that was a bad idea. As I waded vertically in the water, salt water flooded my mouth. The salty water was horrible. I looked around and the distance gave me a mini heart attack. We were so far from the shore. All I could think about was, "What happens if I don't make it? Would that make me a failure?" then I realized that this was just my first stop! I couldn't give up already! So I pushed on. As swells carried me up and down, I felt like I was a surfer. Because the water was murky, you had to look down and swim. I could have sworn it looked red. Maybe it was the sun's reflection? Wait, where was the sun?

The weather was getting worse by the minute as we continued swimming. I was concentrating on my swimming method. The side breathing also allowed me to keep track of my proximity to my Dad. The large swells were making it difficult to execute my strokes as it was like punching into a liquid wall and each and every impact hurt my shoulders. Regular side breathing was a challenge as you could take a mouth full of the Bay if you did not time it right. How could you time your strokes and breathing if the waves were doing the Macarena on you and were totally unpredictable? Should I give up? My grandmother would never give up, and neither would I.

*Waves, Waves everywhere*

We had swam for about half an hour before we got to the middle. Here we paused to gauge the distance and found that the island had fallen some distance behind us with the Golden Gate Bridge and the Bay Bridge on either side. In front of us was the inviting San Francisco skyline shrouded in grey clouds and mist with an occasional flash of lightning. It was a beautiful sight in a cloudy, eerie, crazy way.

Keep in mind, I was also freaking out seeing the lightning. In Colorado, any threat of lightning was taken seriously and no one was allowed in the water till the thunder storm passed and lightning stopped.

As we paused, I could feel the cold water seep into my wetsuit and take away the heat from my body. I looked around and saw the huge swells of sea water coming right at me reminding me that I can't stop for too long. So, I started swimming again.

*The Golden Gate Bridge and the city skyline*

I could see the bright Ghirardelli sign shining bravely through the thick misty air. Oddly, the mist on my head was clearing because I remember hearing another swimmer before we jumped, saying that he was aiming straight for the Ghirardelli lights.

*The Ghirardelli Sign etched in my mind*

I had been swimming for about 50 minutes and was getting tired from fighting the waves and cold by then. The tide seemed to have gotten stronger and picked us up and moved us off course a little. I aimed for a yellow buoy that I spotted at the mouth of the breakwaters. It seemed I was swimming in place and not getting any nearer to the shore. The swells and wind seemed to pick up in intensity and kept pushing back at me. I thought about my cause, my supporters and everyone who was waiting for me on shore giving me strength and courage to complete my swim. I started humming, "Keep on Swimming, Keep on Swimming," from my favorite movie, *Finding Nemo* in which the adorable blue regal tang fish named Dory kept chanting.

When I was about 150 yards away from the finish line, I could hear the crowd yelling and cheering for me from the beach. The excited sea gulls were cheering for me too. A swimmer at the breakwater recognized me and took the time to encourage me on "Come On, Good Job, You can do it, you are Shewli right? The youngest swimmer today, aren't you ?"

I kept swimming until I saw the sand below me, an encouraging sign of being close to shore. A few more strokes and a big wave carried me in as if helping me forward and introducing me to the crowds.

As I stepped out of the water I felt proud of myself knowing that I had escaped from Alcatraz in rough conditions with rain, lightning and thunder to add to my challenge.

I half walked, half dashed out of the water the only thing I could think about was that I had made it. I could hear the remarks about age and knew they were talking about me. It seemed that my facial muscles had frozen and forming words were difficult. As I trudged onto the shore I could feel everyone's eyes on me. A volunteer cut off my timer strap and I was greeted with hugs from my family. People complimented me but I could barely hear anybody as the hum of the waves was still ringing in my head. I knew everyone was around but I couldn't communicate. I was able to muster up a smile of acknowledgement for a few other swimmers but it seemed like a dream. Everything was blurry, my body was aching and the enormity of the feat was slowly just seeping in...

I think my mom hugged me and then I was surrounded by the crowd. I was greeted with a big hug from Lynne Cox and SERC volunteers in red parkas and white hoodies.

As my family, grandparents, parents, brother, uncle, aunt and cousins cheered me on, I received my finisher medal. A flask of warm sweet milk was handed to me and it tasted Yummy!

We walked to the rowing club and I took the hottest shower imaginable. My body didn't feel it though; I was numb from my shoulders down. I walked into the sauna to be greeted by other swimmers - more warm and happy faces. Many asked "How old are you?" Someone knew the answer and replied for me. At this point I was reveling in the hot steamy waters of the shower washing away the cold salty water of the sea. I realized that the sudden cold to hot temperature change was tricking my body into lethargy. I had to consciously prevent myself from falling into a deep sleep right there in the shower. The shower at SERC was very warm and I stayed there for a long time. In the steam room someone said that my lips were purple. I just kept soaking myself in the warmth, humming my favorite song.

Once finished, I was ready for the city of San

Francisco. My parents had site-seeing planned for the rest of the day.

*At Ghirardelli with my grandmother*

After I gained some heat from the humid air, we walked up to Ghirardelli Square. Seeing it through the foggy haze of my swim goggles and my unique vintage point in the water a few hours ago, I couldn't imagine how bright it was up close. Now every time I closed my eyes, the brightness of the sign stained my eyelids. We walked in and saw familiar faces, but that didn't matter to me at all. The vanilla malt sitting right in front of me brought all of my soul and energy back to life. After posing like a celebrity for my parents cameras I attacked the malt had made it disappear in minutes. As I sat savoring the moment, the feeling of fatigue washed over me, meaning that my trip to San Francisco had come to an end and it was time to go home.

    I had swam the inescapable, legendary waters of Alcatraz. I stood up to the challenge and helped spread the word on "Prevention is better than Cure" for breast cancer.

*Super Star*

# 5 TRAINING

In the fall of 2008, my dad swam the Alcatraz with his sister, my aunt Manisha. Looking at the distance they covered got me thinking. At that point I was swimming 1 1/2 miles at practice 4 evenings a week in the pool with my swim team in Denver. I laughed at his speed on that swim to which he asked a question that changed my life, "You think you would like to swim the Alcatraz with me next year?" I said, "Sure, I would swim with you and I bet I am faster than you." When you are asked a question where you choose the outcome, would you choose the wimpy answer?

*Shark Week remains a favorite for us to watch*

A few months later we were watching reruns of Shark Week, when my dad posed the question again about my commitment to swim Alcatraz. He was asking as it was time to register for the 2009 Invitational. Is it a coincidence that we were watching Shark Week when he posed the question? I looked him in the eye and said, "Of course, let's do it."

I was training with my swim team in Denver at this time. I trained and had fun with my friends Savanna, Alex, Abby & Carson. We went to meets almost every Saturday in the summer. Through the winter and spring my parents religiously kept me engaged in swimming by entering me in swim meets and practice. Starting early May, when the snow started melting, dad slowly introduced me to open water swimming. We would take our yellow kayak and visit the nearby lake. We would fish from the shore and walk in the cold waters looking for crawfish. Every now and then we would splash water on each other. We would have a small family outing where my brother and I would get to play in the cold water.

*Kayaking*

Gradually these family picnics by the lake and competitive pool swimming with friends at summer swim became a prelude for my training in open water. My dad taught me the difference of swimming in a lap pool versus open water. At first it was very different and uncomfortable. Being a young kid, I didn't like the thought of putting more effort in swimming, into a skill I thought I knew well. Most Monday and Wednesday evenings, and Saturday mornings my dad and I managed to swim in the Chatfield Reservoir. After a few trips to Chatfield State Park near my house, open water swimming and its technicalities started making sense to me. I began liking open water swimming, getting confident and looking forward to swimming in the lake.

*Gravel Pond*

The designated area in the Chatfield State Park was called the Gravel Pond. At this lake there were no motorized boats allowed and swimming was by permit only. The approximate length of this little lake was 900 meters across, thus a swim across the lake and back would get me close to a mile. What made the gravel pond an amazing place to practice was that it had an island 1/3 the way from the shore (about 300 yards away). This was an excellent distance for me to strive for initially. My dad encouraged me to swim just a short distance to begin with, so I could get acclimatized to the cold, sighting and learning the "ropes" of open water swimming. Interestingly, in a lake you do need to figure out how to deal with the sudden cold, sighting techniques, wind factor, currents and swimming without breaks. Due to my summer swim team I was able to slowly extend my swimming and practice for longer distances.

Oddly, dad never mentioned to me exactly how long was 1.25 miles. I figured it out later those 1.25 miles would be 88 lengths of a 25 yard pool or 22 sets of 100's. I think it was a good thing that he did not try to give me lesson in math about it. The swim might not have happened. Instead, after most swims my dad and I went to feast on delicious Jamba Juice. More than anything, this helped me through the swim practices.

To help me make the commitment to swim 1.5 miles, my dad entered us for the AQUAMAN Open Water Swim and Aquathlon Series. This series of swim/run events is the perfect opportunity for swimmers and triathletes of all ages and abilities to practice their open water swimming in a fun, competitive environment and at distances comfortable to them. Distances for the swim series include a 1/2 mile, 1 mile, 1.5 mile, and 2 mile swim. After the swim, athletes can complete a 5k run. My dad and I opted for the swim series that conducts 6 swims on Tuesdays towards the end of June to the first week of August at the Cherry Creek State Park. This reservoir was also close to my house and allowed us the practice our swimming prowess without having to travel long distances. I gradually increased my swim distance from 1/2 mile to 1.5 miles over the 6 weeks that the events were held. I learned from the swim clinics, usually held just before the race by other swim trainers. Plus I met a lot of really cool people who encouraged me, joked with me and shared some of their experiences. The event organizer Canace Panigutti (Candy) was awesome and very accommodating and supported my efforts all the way. It was so nice to come back every Tuesday and see familiar faces, say hello to new friends and prepare for the swim.

*Cherry Creek State Park*

The swim at the Cherry Creek Reservoir had quite a few elements of open water swimming that I was looking for. The waters were murky and the weather usually was windy causing the water to be cold and choppy. Additionally, there were motor boats and jet skis outside the designated swim area that would kick up waves that made swimming harder. The distances were longer, so you had to put your mind and condition your swim for it. Having other swimmers of varying expertise also helped a lot as I would have companionship and sometimes a little competition going as we would swim close by or pass someone or get passed by a faster swimmer. The after swim ambience was awesome with a masseuse, vendors stalls, food, sport drinks, music and time to catch up with new and old friends about the swim.

It is events like these and organizers like Candy that make the whole experience amazing and you hardly think about the effort of swimming.

I would encourage everyone who is participating in cold temperature open water swimming to definitely consider a trial swim in the same waters as the main event at least a day or two before. The pre-event swims at the Aquatic Park in San Francisco gave me the most confidence to prepare for a cold grueling swim at Alcatraz.

*Pre-Event Swim at the Aquatic Park*

In this next section I wrote about some of the swim techniques that I trained with and modified a little to suit the sea conditions while swimming on race day.

# 6 SWIM TECHNIQUES I USE

Open water swimming can be tricky, and you need strategic thinking, especially when it comes to cold rough and choppy waters with strong tides like I experienced on my first swim on Sept 12, 2009. Knowing how to swim and being able to swim long distances are not enough. Knowing yourself, comprehending reality, having confidence in your strengths and being resourceful is the key. I learned these valuable nuggets of information after jumping from the ferry into the rough cold waters of the San Francisco Bay. Nothing I had done to train for this swim while in Colorado would have prepared me for these tough conditions in California.

In 2009, my family took a vacation in Hawaii where I practiced to swim for the first time long distances in the warm blue ocean. For my first Alcatraz swim, I took off from my school and arrived in San Francisco a week before the event. I acclimatized myself to the waters of Bay with a few practice swims. But none of the preparations compared to the conditions that I faced on the day of the event.

When you can feel all warmth draining out of you and you are in survival mode, you learn fast. On the way you tend to draw from few smart tips discovered by others before you. Here is what I found out.

**Disorientation:** After finishing my first Alcatraz swim, we heard that a few seasoned tri-athletes had to abort the race a few minutes in as they were totally disoriented and were having trouble breathing.

Plunging 6 feet under in cold water can get you disoriented almost immediately as your body naturally reacts to the cold. These several disastrous responses include shivering, constricting blood vessels, increasing metabolism to use more fuel, increasing urine volume, increasing lactate production and decreasing VO2max (volume- oxygen-maximum, the maximum capacity of an individual's body to transport and use oxygen).

We had prepared for this particular effect by always diving into the water head first while practicing in Colorado. My dad insisted on not gradually walking into the lake but train the body with a head first dive and take 25 strong stokes. In addition, we reduced the number of caps and swam in our regular swim suits instead of the wetsuit to be somewhat prepared for the north Californian cold water currents. This method did gave us some understanding of what it would feel to suddenly get shocked with cold water.

**Hyperventilation:** The 8-12 feet jump can cause you to breathe rapidly and deeper than normal, almost pushing you into a panic attack if you are not prepared. Additionally, the cold already starts calling dibs on your exposed body parts like your face, fingers and toes. These body extremities start getting numb and tingly.

Understanding such an obvious bodily reaction, we had decided to bob up to the surface, take a few long breaths, orient ourselves as soon as possible and point to the right direction and start the swim with 25 strong to easy strokes when swimming in the cold sea. This strategy kept our bodies moving and the blood circulating while the strong swim stokes moved us forward towards our destination.

**Swimming in High Swells and Stormy Conditions:** Imagine transitioning from swimming in the controlled environments of a pool and the glassy surface of a lake or a sheltered bay to 10 foot swells, erratic winds and a fast tide. Add to that a wisp of a girl who is disoriented and going through the hyperventilation stages. Almost makes you scream, "Get that little girl out of the water." I am glad no one got that idea and fished me out. I would have missed out on the greatest experience of my life (so far).

Instead of swimming hard into the waves and towards my destination, I slowed down into a rhythmic breast stroke and starting laying down my modified plan of action. After swimming a few stokes, I could see that although the winds were erratic, the waves seem to have a rhythm about them. I tried a few short strokes and they seem to be half successful. While I got slapped on my face with walls of water on the other half of the strokes. These are not light smacks to your face; instead, they are a full-bodied, totally-enveloping slap to your face that shakes you completely. I modified my strokes a little more to allow me to glide further and streamlined my bodyline in the water.

**Breathing:** Breathing was the main part of the swim that allowed me to calm down my anxieties and continue swimming well. I tried various techniques I had learned like breathing every 5 strokes, sight and breathe. But with 10 feet high swells, all bets and trainings are off. Every time you turn your head to get a mouth full of air, you may be slammed with a mouthful of salty seawater. It was really hard to time the breathing intervals. I tried repeatedly to make some sense out of it but it was almost impossible. I decided to change my breathing stance by rotating my hips and body so I can get higher in the water before taking a breath. And it worked. I started maintaining just a little reserve in my lungs before taking a quick gasp of air, just in case there was a swell that prevented me from breathing. I also started timing the waves to synchronize my breathing with every third wave. This approach worked most of the time but not always it gave me some comfort and some real good opportunities for taking deep breaths.

**Swimming Straight and Sighting:** I had trained myself to swim straight by learning how to keep my arms straight while swimming and keeping my arms extended straight out from the shoulder. Like dropping a letter into a post box.

I always found breathing first and sighting later took too much effort and was confusing. I had combined my breathing and sighting so I would sight first and then take a breath. I could do this at every 3 to 5 strokes. This method allows me to carry my stroke momentum through the sighting.

At times when the swell was too large, I would switch to separate sighting and breathing cycles and that worked to.

Another method is finding a buddy: If you swim alongside a lead swimmer, you do not have to lift your head so often to navigate. But be cautious about following just anyone who swims by. In my case it was my dad and me who switched roles navigating to give the other some rest.

From the time we got our instructions at the SERC by the race director, all the swimmers knew that they must sight on tall buildings and structures to the left of the Aquatic Park to swim a path that counters the currents and the wind. Orienting to large and high structures allows for a straighter swim and by constantly checking on your bearings you can determine whether you need to course correct. Look for big and high structures. Bigger the better. Also, higher the waves, needs more sighting.

**It Is Ok To Stop and Reorient Yourself?** Unless you are trying to break the world record, take the time every now and then to pause and look around. Make sure you are heading in the direction you are trying to go. A lot of swimmers, me included, get so caught up with the act of swimming that going off course especially on a foggy morning with poor visibility is easy.

**Definitely Pause To See the Most Beautiful Sight Ever:** When you are halfway through the swim, and if you have a kind of clear day, pause to see how the Alcatraz Island has fallen behind you. Look to either side and you will see the Golden Gate Bridge and the Bay Bridge from a very unique view (at sea level). Think of the escapees from the Alcatraz and how they would have felt to have gotten away from the prison and were so close to freedom. Of course the few that escaped would have done so at night and were seeing the city lights and the Alcatraz Island lighthouse lights. I think.

**Sight Adjustments:** Sighting off one set of structures is not enough when swimming the Alcatraz. After you get to almost 3/4 of the way, you need to re-evaluate your trajectory and re-adjust to another set of structures that will guide you past the breakwaters of the Aquatic Park. The idea is to let the current carry you to the breakwater and once at the breakwater, you can make a dash for the beach. This approach works great for most swimmers who don't swim at 5 mph and are scenic swimmers like me.

For those who plan on swimming the Alcatraz, pay close attention to the orientation where officials will advise you to re adjust your sighting references when close to the Liberty Ship SS Jeremiah O'Brien If you miss your orientation, ask the volunteers on the ferry and they will guide you.

# 7 EQUIPMENT CHECK

I have included some detailed training suggestions based upon my experience of open water swimming. Some of this content is from the sound advice sent via email to all SERC swimmers prior to the swim.

**Wetsuits:** Most newbies, like me wear a wetsuit. I would say that if you are planning to swim in 55 °FF-62 °F water and you have no access to practice in such cold water, you may want to consider a good wetsuit. It is imperative that you try it and swim in it a few times PRIOR to race day to ensure it still fits properly, a wetsuit that is too tight will mean you have trouble expanding your chest to take in a full breath. Folks at the SERC say that every year they have new swimmers that jump from the boat and the first words the rescuers hear is "I can't breathe."

Make sure your wetsuit fits; there are lots of places that rent wetsuits if you need a different size, and go for a training swim wearing the wetsuit, leave nothing to chance, make sure your equipment works for you, not against you.

**Put the rubber to the pool:** Try out a brand-new wetsuit in the pool before using it in open water. Even with a wetsuit you already own, wear it for a few pool practices before a race. The pool provides a safe and comfortable environment to adjust for the way the wetsuit changes your feel for the water and body position. However, check with the manufacturer first to make sure the chemicals in the pool won't deteriorate the wetsuit material. It will be uncomfortable at first, but you get used to it.

Diving wetsuits are difficult to swim in so consider renting a thinner suit made for swimming.

**Anti-Chaffing:** Use Vaseline or body glide to coat areas like all-around the neck, arm pits and legs and any other areas where there could be a possibility of chaffing. Swimming with a wetsuit rubbing against your neck is very uncomfortable and is totally avoidable.

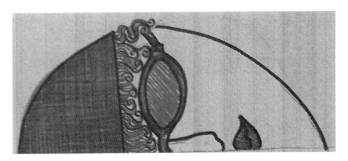

**Goggles:** Try out your goggles and make sure they seal (you don't want to be looking out of half full goggles and having to take them off time after time to see as your sighting is very important for this swim). If they seal and are comfortable, then the next thing is to clean them with warm soapy water to get all of the oil and dirt off of them. On the night before the swim put a drop of dish detergent or baby shampoo on the inside and smear it around and wash it off clean. This will keep the goggles from fogging while swimming you can also put a drop of baby shampoo in the lenses and clean the day of the swim rinsing with water.

Some use an anti-fogging spray or use a coating of saliva for anti-fogging. I have used both and they work for me. I also take the time in the middle of my swim to wash and rinse my goggles so I get a break, re-orient and clear any mist that may have accumulated.

When you jump off the boat, depending on how you land, your goggles may be ripped off your head so you may want to put a hand over them or as some swimmers do is put the goggles around their neck and then pull them up their head when they are clear of boat (Try jumping off a diving board or off a pier and see what works best).

**Ear Plugs:** Most South Enders use Mack's Earplugs to keep the cool water out of our ears and have found that they mold to your ears well. Bring an extra set just to be sure you have enough for your practice swims as well as the main event.

**Cap and or Thermal Cap?** If you prefer to swim in skins (no wetsuit) you might consider wearing a thermal cap as there is heat loss through the head and you will stay warmer wearing one. Try it out ahead of time as you may also be asked to wear the event stipulated caps over the thermal cap. Check for comfort too.

**Training Suggestions:** Keep practicing continuous swimming wherever you have a pool or open water for $1\frac{1}{2}$ to 2 miles or 60 to 90 minutes, with some speed work built in to help with any cross currents we may experience when crossing from Alcatraz to Aquatic Park.

Try swimming with the gear you will be using the day of the event, ahead of time.

When swimming in open water try working on your sighting without raising your head fully out of the water. Just take a peek over forward and look out on your breathing side to help orient you. Try swimming toward a hill or tree in the distance.

**Blind Leading the Blind:** Don't follow the swimmer in front of you as they may be zigzagging or going in circles. Know where you are swimming, feel the direction of the swells and adjust your swim course.

**Nutrition before The Swim:** Eat a high quality protein meal and veggies the night before the swim. It is usually recommended to have a hearty meal before swimming in the Bay. Something I like-a big bowl of steel cut oats or pasta a couple of hours before my swim that gives a slow release of energy (complex carbohydrates) for the duration of a swim like this.

Consider hydrating yourself with fluids about 2 days ahead of time with fluids having Cytomax or Maltodextrin or just plain water before walking down to the boat or your event this helps the body to stay hydrated while you go through extreme exercise for a long period of time...

If you think you will be in the water for more than 45 minutes you may consider stuffing a pack of GU in your suit and using it through the swim. Finally, do your research of the area, weather, water temperature, tides and the facilities available before and after the swim. By visualizing your swim beforehand you will find various questions that need to be answered either from the event website or from the race coordinators.

# 8 COOL THINGS I DID AT THE BAY

During my swims I had the opportunity to meet some of the coolest people ever. I got a chance to chat with Lynne Cox who was the chief guest on my first swim.

*Lynne signing her book "Antarctica" for me in 2009*

Lynne is perhaps best known for swimming the Bering Strait in 1987, from the island of Little Diomede in Alaska to Big Diomede, then part of the Soviet Union, where the water temperature averaged around 4 °C (40 °F). At the time people living on the Diomede Islands—only 3.7 km (2.3 miles) apart—were not permitted to travel between them. Her accomplishment was instrumental in easing Cold War tensions as Ronald Reagan and Mikhail Gorbachev both praised her success.

*After my race with Lynne and my brother Shiv in 2009*

If you were to ever want to read an inspiring book, I would highly recommend Lynne's book *Swimming to Antarctica* and *Grayson*. She was always the slowest swimmer in her swim classes. She rose far above her swim class standards by practice and hard work. She has twice held the record for the fastest crossing (men or women) of the English Channel (1972 in a time of 9h 57 mins and 1973 in a time of 9h 36 mins). Imagine this, she has the asteroid 37588 Lynnecox named in her honor.

In 2010, I got to hang out with Jackie and Dave. Jackie Cobell has become the slowest person to swim the English Channel. In a heroic effort that took 28 hours and 44 minutes to cross from Dover to Calais. She comfortably beat the previous world record holder. Her husband Dave is also an English Channel swimmer. I loved their English accent. Dave promptly gave me $20 for my cause. Both were such wonderful people. They always made me laugh with their unassuming humorous spin on things.

I liked what I read in the news about Jackie. One British tabloid wrote, "I had no watch in the water so I just swam and swam and had absolutely no idea of the time," said Mrs. Cobell, from Tonbridge, Kent.

*With Jackie and Dave Cobell in 2010*

Visiting the Bay area always gives me an opportunity to visit with my cousins Samir and Viraj. I get to hang out with them and play their video games. They take every opportunity to have me try their favorite restaurants. As we all share a love for Sushi we go to as many places as possible where they serve unlimited Sushi. On my visit in 2012, we stopped by Tommy's Joynt at Van Ness and Geary for a taste of their turkey.

I get to hear stories about their school pranks, share songs that are new and watch hilarious movies. I love the view     of     the     Bay     from     their     deck.

*Goofing off prior to our swim in 2010*

My cousins liked the idea of swimming Alcatraz, so we made it a family affair and swam it together

*Pictured after our 2012 Alcatraz swim*

*Samir taking first prize for Under 14 category in 2010*

*From the left, Manisha, Samir, Viraj, dad and me in 2010*

While in San Francisco we did the usual touristy things that it's famous for. We visited as many points of interest from nearby Carmel to Napa Valley, Muir Woods to Sausalito. Of all the places, Fisherman's Warf was always a highlight.

*From the Left, Viraj, me and Samir after our 2012 swim*

Among the free things we liked were watching the fishing boats, sightseeing boats, ferry charters, sea lions basking in the sun, street performers, visiting art galleries, caricature artists, spray-paint artists, the Spy Shop, and watching the Boudin's bakers make sourdough French bread shaped as animals.

It was funny to watch the Segway tours go by in a line with people standing on scooter-like vehicles and driving/gliding by a touch of their hands or leaning in any one direction. I think it would have been fun to ride one myself. Maybe when I am a little older and can reach up to the handle.

We enjoyed visiting the historic ships, tugs and ferries on the San Francisco maritime National Historical Park on the Hyde Street Pier. We also visited the SS JEREMIAH O'BRIEN on Pier 45

*With my aunt Manisha and dad at Hyde Street Pier*

We drove up to the Golden Gate Bridge and peeked over to see the entire bay and also visited the Golden Gate Park.

We loved watching chocolate being made at Ghirardelli. Drinking a hot chocolate took on a different meaning after that chocolate making tour.

*Brownies, Cookies, and my brother Shiv at Ghirardelli*

The trips that we enjoyed the most were the ferry ride to the Alcatraz Island and visiting the now decommissioned prison. We had watched the movie *Escape from Alcatraz*, *The Rock* and *The Bird Man* prior to visiting the prison and it was re-living history.

It was fun to browse around souvenir shops and a few knick knacks for ourselves and for friends. We would take breaks at the sea food stalls on Taylor Street where you would find steaming crab cauldrons, seafood restaurants, and street vendors selling every kind of fried seafood, fish and chips, soups and chowders. We loved the shrimp, oysters and sour dough bowls of clam chowder.

The restaurants that we liked the most were the Scoma's Restaurant where I had my first Shirley Temple and the freshest salmon ever.

At night we dined at the McCormick & Culet a seafood Restaurant in San Francisco's historic Ghirardelli Square. We sat facing the Alcatraz Island and the beautiful calm sea. You could hear the lonely fog horn in the distance. We also dined at the Cioppino's where we met with other friends after my swim.

*To sum it all*

Parking close to the Aquatic Park and for free is close to impossible. A known secret is parking at Van Ness where the historic F-Line streetcar and two cable car lines terminate. Four hour parking is available for visits the Aquatic Park. Walking along side Van Ness you could continue to the very end of the break water and see locals fishing and crabbing. This was an excellent spot to just take in the bay area by watching large merchant ships, sail boats, ferries and motor boats in the channel. A lazy walk over the small hill takes you to Pier 3 where we came across a farmers market with delectable local produce such as fresh peaches, honey and cheeses.

# 9 SOUTH END ROWING CLUB (SERC)

Formed in 1873, solely for the purpose of rowing, the South End Rowing Club is an institution. It has expanded to include swimming, handball, and running as club sponsored sports. This club is more historical, and less state-of-the-art. I can just imagine that the club has a membership roster and visitors of the who's-who from around the world. Interestingly, this exclusive club opens its doors for day use for visitors for a nominal fee on Wednesdays and Fridays.

A visit inside the club shows laminated wooden rowing boats like the Viking boats, the Valhalla, the Valkyrie, the

Thor, and the Whitehall Sal Reina, all stowed with care in a very vintage setting. All around there are photographs that date to the beginning of the club in 1873. A close inspection will immediately transport you into the beginnings of the San Francisco Bay area, its sea faring industry with merchant ships, fishing boats, street life and vendors of bygone days.

In all my visits to the SERC club, no one ever asked me if I was a member of the club. On knocking on the door, the first thing you may encounter is a smiling face of a club member ready to include you in the family of the rowing club. In the dim lights inside the club, you may see other club members working on restoring a boat or busy with the upkeep of the club. Something else I noticed that the dress code was casual and there was a lot of camaraderie and healthy bit of leg pulling amongst club members. I loved the warm comforting feel of this historical two storied building. And always hope that someday I could be a contributing member at SERC.

## A Tribute to Bill Wygant

My dad met Bill who was then the Race Director of the SERC Alcatraz Invitational swim, in 2008. In his conversation he asked Bill whether SERC would allow a young girl of ten to swim in the race. That conversation paved the way for me to swim the Alcatraz Invitation thrice.

Bill was very optimistic about a ten year old swimming a distance that even adults dreamt of undertaking. His only concern was that this should be a safe and positive experience for me.

*Bill Wygant and me in 2010*

Bill asked that my current swim coach provide a letter of recommendation for me and insisted that my dad or a coach swim with me. I can't comprehend the hoops that Bill had to jump through to get the insurance companies to approve and underwrite a ten year old swimmer. But Bill had that part well-handled and there was never any doubt that SERC would sanction my swim.

I am proud to say that due to our efforts and positive results, SERC created a special age category for "fourteen and under" like me from 2011. Now most kids can enter by their guardians signing a special waiver online. SERC has also created a special prize category for fourteen and under kids.

I wanted to take this opportunity to thank Bill Wygant, his awesome club of willing volunteers, the brave underwriters and SERC for making this adventure possible.

# 10 BLOG & IN THE NEWS

The news media covered my swim before and after the event and made me feel like a super star for a while. You can find all of these video/recordings/references on my blog: **HTTP://SHEWLI.BLOGSPOT.COM**

## Television

7News has been a constant supporter of my efforts to contribute and make a difference for cancer patients and spread the word on Breast Cancer Prevention.

Thank you to **Doug Schepman**, **Christine Chang, Bertha Lynn, Mike Landess** and the **7News crew**

## Radio

Every week the KYGO Kelly & Rider Mornings Show recognized people in our community that are doing amazing things.

Thank you **Rider** for interviewing me. I loved the Jaws music theme in the background

## Print and Online News & Social Media

Local, National and International news carried my story and even my friends and neighbors helped bring awareness for my events. *The Voice, The Herald, Milonee-Tulikolom, Platte River Academy*, and *India Abroad* supported me.

Thank you everyone and a specially **Sonya Ellingboe, Chris Michlewicz** and **Suman Guha Mozumder** for writing about my cause.

**Sponsors**

I was sponsored by *DonnaBellas Angels, invVEST*, and *Whole Foods Market Highlands Ranch.*

In 2010, I dedicated my swim to a cause that was close to my heart. A cause making a tangible difference in the lives of cancer patients while in therapy. I collaborated with my mother and DonnaBellas Angels (a not for profit organization) providing 'My Angel' therapeutic aids for cancer patients. Details: **www.donnabellasangels.org**

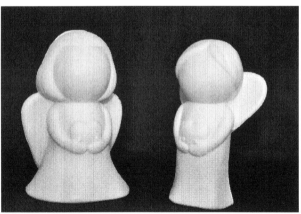

*'My Angel'*

'My Angel' are cute boy and girl angel figurines made of soft stress-relieving foam, created and designed by my mother Shohini Ghosh, for Cancer patients going through severe therapy.

# ABOUT THE AUTHOR

Shewli Ghosh is a thirteen year old girl living in Littleton, Colorado USA. In 2009, at age 10, she swam a distance of 1.25 mile from the Alcatraz Island to the San Francisco Bay. She followed it with 2 more successful swims in 2010 and 2012.

Shewli enjoys writing, traveling, trying out different cuisines and loves an adrenalin rush. In the years to come, she would like to continue to grow in her creative skills, athletic abilities, and help others achieve similar goals.

*Shewli Ghosh 2012*

Made in the USA
Middletown, DE
26 November 2018